AFTER THE STORM
NOW WHAT?

MARY THOMPSON

Copyright © 2021 Mary Thompson
All rights reserved.

No part of this book may be reproduced or transmitted in any form or by any means, electronic or mechanical, including photocopying and recording, or by any information storage and retrieval system, without permission in writing from the publisher: Mary Thompson

Printed in the United States of America

ISBN: 978-0-578-88389-2

DEDICATION

First, to God who gave me a mind to think to write this book. Then, I would like to dedicate this word to my daughter-in-law, Tamara Thompson, who is always patient in helping me in so many ways. And to her husband, Joe Thompson, for letting me borrow his wife for three months. I also would like to give thanks and glory to God for my beautiful children, who are always by my side to motivate me and lift me and say, "mama, you can do this!" So, to you, Delita, Cindy, Detrajo, Kinsey, Joe and Charity, for being there for me; mother loves you all.

CONTENTS

Acknowledgments 1

Chapter 1: Comparison Between Physical
And Spiritual Storms 3

Chapter 2: The Storm Is Passing Over 17

Chapter 3: Strong Storms In The Midst Of
A Divorce 29

Chapter 4: Storms Overturning Your Finances 43

Chapter 5: Quietness In The Storm Of Loneliness........... 55

Chapter 6: Climate Change In The Storm Of
Mental Health 65

Chapter 7: Thunderstorms In Life/Sunshine
In Death 73

Chapter 8: After The Storm, Now What?......................... 89

Chapter 9: Now What? Continue… 99

Chapter 10: After The Storm, There Is A Pot Of
Gold At The End Of The Rainbow.................................. 109

Chapter 11: Finally, The End Of The Storms................. 121

ACKNOWLEDGMENTS

I acknowledge God in all my ways so he can direct my prayers. I plunder in my heart about the storm that people have to face but don't know what to do. I have been in some storms, but I thank God that he brought me out. Who do you want to go to amid your storm? Sometimes mistrust causes people not to share anything with anybody. Everyone has a storm in their life, but how do you handle them? Do you go to God? Or do you try to go through the storm alone? We all need each other, so this book is to help you do out with the old and bring in the new.

I am grateful for my loving family and friends who gave me a lot of support as I began to write my third book. I appreciate you all for your love and support. Special thanks to Darlene Milan and Deborah Smith, who believed in me, who I could talk to at any time. Thanks also to publisher Dennard Mitchell for teaching me so much about publishing my third book, "After the Storm, Now What?"

CHAPTER 1

COMPARISON BETWEEN PHYSICAL AND SPIRITUAL STORMS

There are many storms, physical and spiritual.

Let's talk about a few storms for a minute. There are many natural storms of life such as tornadoes, hurricanes, earthquakes, snowstorms, sand storm, derechos, flooding, hailstorms, ice storms, lightning and thunderstorms, and tropical storms. Let me explain how life is compared with natural storms. Let's compare nature and spiritual storms (1 Cor. 1:27) "but hath chosen the foolish things of the world to confound the wise; and God hath chosen the weak things of the world to confound the things which are mighty." Jesus used parables to explain things about life so we could understand things better. You see, I am a visual learner, so I need to see it. First, you just can't tell me or lecture me and think I should understand what you are teaching. I appreciate Jesus' teaching in the parable; it helps me understand my life and the changes that I have gone through. As you go through many things, you will learn more and more. When it is explained better, even a fool will understand. Let's look at some of the parables Jesus taught so that we can understand and recognize the different storms in your life that are devastating, hard, heartbreaking, viscous, and overwhelming. Let's look at some of Jesus parables:

1. Parable of the lost sheep. Luke 15:1-7
2. Parable of the lost coin Luke 15:8-10
3. Parable of the lost son Luke 15:11-32

All were told to let you know and understand that a soul was lost and angels rejoiced over a lost soul saved because of repentance. Jesus taught naturally so that a person could understand better. You can understand life's story better if explained with examples that are mainly read and taught. God's word tells us to write the vision and make it plain (Habakkuk 2:2). Some of our storms are so hard that we think we can't make it through. Some are hard and unpredictable, and we do not know when they will come. They can look like they are happening right after each other, and you don't even know why it is all happening. It looks like things are not going to end, but God wants you to hold on. He is right there with you. It doesn't mean he doesn't love you. We don't understand it. We don't know why we keep doing the same thing over and over again. Financially, we can't keep up with bills when we get behind. We rob Peter to pay Paul (an old saying). We don't see it until it's too late, and we need professional help to get back on track. That is the way Derecho storms are—winds blowing everywhere repeatedly. Then we have flood storms due to rainstorms when the water rises faster than it can drain, leaving buildings and roads underwater and damaging homes and properties. That's the way storms affect marriages; things get so bad that they wreck lives and families. The husbands and wives can't handle it any longer, so they seek divorce. Everything is torn up and damaged. Sometimes this happens because we do not count the cost to see if it is our soulmate, we jump too quickly because of lust, and we keep repeating the same mistake over and over again. We need God's help in our life; he's there; just talk to him. He is not so far that he cannot be reached; (Isa59:1) "behold, the Lord's hand he is not shortened, that it cannot save; neither his ear heavy, that it cannot hear." God is there for you if only you believe. He wants to help you. Some thunderstorms can cause a wide range of different types of weather. I would like to think of thunderstorms as loneliness because they can come from anywhere, damaging our thinking and health and causing bitterness because of the lack of attention from others. Although we feel helpless, God is still there. We have to recondition our minds to believe that God knows what we are going through. Elijah felt he was so alone with no one to help him that he wanted to die, but if you read God's words in 1 King 19:4-8, God tells us to bring our burden to him. I feel like this is when lightning strikes; it's like the devil tries us and tries to destroy us naturally. This is a dry storm where there is no rain, and it causes a wildfire. The devil is real, don't be fooled; he strikes when we are down and out. Look towards God right now! Elijah had what we would call wilderness thinking; it can do damaging things (like lightning). We become discouraged, hindered by our own minds. And if we are not careful, it can destroy us. Get professional help, like talking to your pastor, a counselor, a best friend you can trust. There is help in the storms. Then you have storms that are powerful and dangerous, like tornadoes and hurricanes; they have high winds, heavy rain and storms with surges and swells. The high winds carry debris that can fall on you and kill you. It is like unexpected trouble coming from every cause, and you feel like you want to question God, but you don't know how or even if you should. It's OK to ask; just how do you ask? That's what matters. Take, for example, Elizabeth and Zechariah and Mary and Joseph in the Bible. Mary pondered things in her heart—she ponders about having a child and not being touched by men, she just said, "how could this be?" Whereas Zechariah asked the question the wrong way to get his answers. When it was time for Elizabeth to have her son, and he was to be named John, Zechariah didn't understand why he had to name his son John. There's nothing wrong with asking God; He wants to give you comfort. God had to close Zechariah's mouth until the baby was born. (Luke 1:5-25, 57-66) The storms will come and go. Death will come, but there will be life after. When the storm of life came upon Jesus and they took his life, He rose again (death could not hold him down). Just hold on! (Matt 25:53) Through the storms of life, we shall live again.

1. God will call the dead, and they shall rise to receive eternal life in glory.
2. Dead bodies will be changed into an immortal form
3. They will seek God face to face.

The physical storms will return later, and spiritually, you will die but be raised to live again. Some of the physical warning signs for storms include the way clouds form, temperature drop from cold to warm, warm to cold, and darkness in thunderstorms. Have you ever watched animals? How do they react? The birds, the cows, the sheep and the horses, how do they react? There is also a warning spiritually; hanging around toxic people, not recognizing how God is working in your life, not reading your Bible, not praying. Your discipleship slowly goes away because of a lack of your faith.

There are warnings about physical storms, but people do not recognize them. Physical storms tear up almost everything; if you can see by reading, there are signs that I have given you. You don't have to go through these storms alone. Hold on! I have to say this because as you are reading this book, Satan will try you in all kinds of ways, just like the physical storms in this world that travel north, south, east, west. You need to know the warning signs. The spiritual storms will attack as well; in our bodies, health, mind, home, business, and relationships. Warning comes before destruction for God's people, so let's watch for the physical storms as well as spiritual storms.

Scripture for storms

Ezek 33:5

Ez7:25

Jere 4:20

Job 26:6

Rom 3:11

Ps. 10:14

Joel 1:15

Jere 50:22

Ez 3:17

Ez 33:4

Job 21:30

Is13:6

Ps.35:8

Is:10:2

Prov 15:1

Ps. 88:11

Colo 1:28

Job 2:20

I hope this will help you understand the spiritual storms through the physical storms; both are devastating.

How many physical storms do you know? Describe them:

_____

_____

_____

_____

_____

_____

_____

_____

_____

_____

"Clouds come floating into my life, no longer to carry rain or usher storms, but to add color to my sunset sky."

- Rabindranath Tagore

CHAPTER 2

THE STORM IS PASSING OVER

When my granddaughter would come into the room and see her mother crying, "what's wrong, mom?" she would say. "Nothing, dear," her mother would reply. Then she would pat her mother on the back and say, "it's going to be alright, mom." Coming from a little girl, this is so sweet. I was told time and time the sun will shine just before dark. We sometimes don't understand how life can deal us a bad or good hand. I'm reminded of the story about Jesus' disciples. They found Jesus in the hidden part of the ship, asleep on a pillow, and awoke him to say to him, "Master, carest not that we perish?" (Mark 4:37-38)

This God is very concerned about us. All Jesus had to say is "peace, be still," and the wind ceased, and there was a great calmness (Mark 4:39). Let's realize that we do have a helper, just trust God! God wants us to call out for help. When storms come, let's not fear. Jesus tells us to fear not, but I am with you; be not dismayed, for I am God; I will strengthen you, I will help you, I will uphold you with my righteous right hand (Isaiah 41:10). Sometimes, the storms seem to last a long time and you feel that it will never end. The storm that Paul was in when they arrested him and sailed out from Crete did not appear to be heavy, but sometimes the storm seems light, then it gets worse; that is the way life gets with some of us. The ones that were on the boat thought they were going to fall into quicksand and sink; that is the way it is with someone with a critical illness such as cancer, leukemia, lupus, etc., all hope seems to be taken away. Paul stood amid everyone on the boat and said, "yeah, we should have hearkened unto me and not have left Crete, and to have gained this harm and loss." Sometimes, we need to think before we react. Some people believe in God but want to wait before going to the doctor because of their faith in God. Yet, God initiated doctors to help us, so I advise you to go to the doctor. It is good to have faith that God will heal, and I know because he healed me from MS, but I didn't delay getting help; I checked it out, else this is a storm that could have been long-lasting. "BUT GOD" was with me always. Paul exhorted them to be of good cheer and that there will be no loss of any man's life among you but of this ship (Act 27: 21). God is with you in the storm; just hang on. Read Acts 27:23 - 26 to see how God was with

Paul and the others. Just like in the story, God can turn your situation around. I told my granddaughter that she would have to learn to pray so she can help her mother when the bad times come, and she said, "but I don't know how." I told her how to pray and what to say and explained that she is just talking to God like she would talk to me. There is nothing that God doesn't know; we all go through something, and God knows what we face. The sun will shine again! There is a song that goes like this, "there is a storm over the ocean, and it is headed this way; if you are not anchored in Jesus, you will surely drift away." Have faith and believe God will help you. Not your will but Christ's will; he cares about you. Give God your heart and realize the storm won't last long. My grandson made a statement "that when he gets over his trouble, he should have learned from it and be able to stand." I asked my grandson, "after you have gone through and other things come up against you, then what?"

He replied that he would go on to the next level. He will not quit because with every disappointment comes a higher and higher level of letdowns; they come and go, but how you handle it helps you be a conqueror with God. I told him that I never thought of it that way. We can do all things through Christ Jesus, who strengthens us (Romans 8:31). I like the response that I got from him as we do not just crawl up in a hole and die there. Like the old saying, "if someone throws you a lemon, make lemonade." The thing with you is that you have to be determined with your faith that you can overcome (Hebrews 11:1). Have faith and determination with your mind that you will go far. When it seems dark, God is there. I know this because he has always been with me when I didn't know what to do. He always sends someone to give comfort, start paying attention, and you will see. When God's disciples entered the ship and went to Capernaum, it was dark. The storms are real, and it gets dark in our life sometimes that we need a release. I am sure you have heard someone make the statement, "The sun will rise just before day." It means that you don't have to worry much longer because the sun comes up just before day. There was a relief when the disciples were in the boat and the sea was rising up because of the heavy wind blowing (John 7:16), But God hallelujah! All we can say is "But God." He came to the disciples' aid on the sea. God will come to us just in time; sometimes, it's hard to believe, but that's when we have to have faith in God (John 6:19-20). We have to put our trust in God even when it seems difficult. Jesus said, "it is I; be not afraid," after he sensed that they were frightened. I told my grandson that you just have to trust God, and he stated that he understood. I want to tell you that if you have faith as a grain of mustard seed, you can say to the mountain be removed into the sea (Matthew 17: 20). Talk to God about your problems; He will hear you and answer. Build your faith. There are many scriptures in the Bible that will help you. I want to ask you, where is your faith? (Luke 8:25)

God can calm the sea, and I know he can help whatever problems you are having, whether sickness, finances, racism, divorce, or loneliness. We are told we will suffer a while, but it will make us stronger; keep the faith. God is in control. But the God of grace, who has called us unto his eternal glory by Christ Jesus after that you had suffered a little while, made you perfect—stabilizing, strengthening and settling you (1 Peter 5:10). God is with you in this storm, and if you believe, he will bring you out. We have to remember trusting in God is our base of faith. We must continue to read God's word to bring us out. There is a lot of thunder and lightning in the storm but believe that the storm is passing over. Watch for the son; he is coming with the clouds.

Listen to these testimonies:

I am a living witness of what God can do when storms come my way. I live daily with two diseases—lupus for 25 years and interstitial lung disease for 18 years; this is an immune system disease. I exercise, drink plenty of water and trust God because my healing comes from him. I am doing great. I do not let negative thoughts come; they are not included in my health. I was diagnosed by a physician, but that's not what my God tells me. I fully trust in God for my health and well-being. Julia Gauthia, Jackson, TN.

December 16, 2018, this time last year, I was in a dark place. Depressed was an understatement. December 19, 2018, was the day the doctor predicted my demise. He gave me six months to live and said, more than likely, I would be back in less than ten days, DOA! Nothing but God! I am so happy I am still here. Yay! That was two years ago; August 7 made one year that I graduated from the hospital. I had minor and major setbacks along the way. I am still going through it. But God! I've fought every day. I will never give up. God has plans for my life. Amen. I shall not die but live and declare the works of the Lord (Psalms 118:7). Tammy Thompson, Lansing, MI 48917

If you are going through one of life's storms or what seems like an unending road, you may not feel like you will even experience a sunny day. The sun does shine just before dawn if you can believe it. I have lived a long time and always heard that saying, and it is true. It just seems like it will never come. That's why you need to build your faith. You can make it through the storm. The storm helps to build character and strengthen you because God is with you. ("And not only so, but we glory in tribulations also: knowing that tribulation worketh patience; And patience, experience; and experience, hope," Rom 5:3-4).

What is your Storm that destroys everything, and how did you handle it?

Notes

"Worry does not empty tomorrow of its troubles. It empties today of its strength."
- Corrie Ten Boom

CHAPTER 3

STRONG STORMS IN THE MIDST OF A DIVORCE

"I want a divorce," said John. But he got no response from his wife, so the day went on. The next day, the husband said, "you don't believe me, do you?" So, his wife said, "no, I don't think you are playing; I just don't care what you want." This went on for several months until Sarah, his wife, was at home sick one day and said, "OK, you want a divorce? Let's go! I will give you what you want." They both went to the lawyer's office and filed for a divorce. It didn't have to do with a woman or a man; they just grew apart.

Another scenario of a divorce is Bill. Bill was a man that took care of everything for his wife, but she was not satisfied. They had one child together. It was a deal of a divorce—Bill had to take his wife to court to get custody of his child. Bill's wife just wanted to be free. She was involved with another man and was attracted to the other man's money. The idea that Bill's wife wanted to leave left him very stressed until he had to get counseling. He still has feelings for his wife. It's a hard pill to swallow, but God. Bill believes in God, but he also knows you can't make anyone love you. He is going on with his life at this time.

Jack is another man who's just tired of being with his wife, Jean. Jack wanted Jean to go everywhere with him, but this made her so tired as she had no life. Jean stayed single for years after they got a divorce. She cried at night because she thought she could have done something to keep her marriage together. After crying for months, Jean said she heard God tell her to get up, "you have had your pity party; now get up and do something with your life." And that is what Jean did. She built a life for herself. She went to college and got a degree in social work to help someone else going through the same thing. Now she began her new life.

These are stories that I got from interviewing people about their divorce. It was not easy to talk about it, but they agree that life was beginning all over for them. They did not want to give their name, so I kept it as unknown and put this in my book so that you can realize that men and women go through storms—a bitter marriage and separating—but there is life after, there is a new beginning. Believe it or not, this means that men hurt too. They just hold it in and don't let anyone know while a woman is more emotional. I have an opportunity to learn about emotional pain in both men and women. I talked to several people about this. Both men and women stated that they had to talk to a therapist to get their life back together. Talking to these people, there were many reasons for the divorce, but life goes on. It's not over for you. God gives grace for everything; the Bible stated that every way of a man is right in his own eyes, but the Lord pondereth the hearts (Proverbs 21:2I). I was taught in the church I went to that it was a sin to divorce, but God does not want us to live a miserable life. When a man has taken a wife, and it comes to pass that she no longer has favor in his eyes, she was given a bill of divorcement (Deuteronomy 24:2); but there was a reason. Read it for yourself to get an understanding of that scripture. There are reasons for divorce, such as fornication (Matt.19:8). The thing is, after the divorce, now what? You do not have to continue in guilt. "I wonder what I could have done to make my marriage right. If I could have done something different, I thought maybe the guilt wouldn't have followed me for a long time. I had to get deliverance of some kind; if it had not been for God, I feel I would still have guilt and been in misery." It is not for us to continue to blame ourselves. It is over, so live; be the best you! God does not want you to be a punching board or the one giving and not receiving love back. He put us together to be one. But because of the hardness of man's heart, it is not. A house divided against itself can't stand (Matt. 12:22-28). Look for something you like doing, like going to college, and learning a different career, drawing, writing—whatever you like and want to do that you've wanted to do all your life. Love yourself like going to the spa and getting your hair done. Seek God for guidance (Matt. 6:33). Life goes on; you can make it. If you will it in your mind, you can do it! Do not let divorce set you back from living; make it happen. This is for both men and women, especially for the men whose wives have left them and the children for another man. Believe me, men are hurting too! There are lessons after the rainbow! Don't spend life moping around in the same limbo every day. Get counseling, talk it out and get your children counseling. That is your responsibility. NOW WHAT? Guess what! Real life goes on. No matter what causes a divorce, it is never easy for anyone. Both suffer; believe it or not. It's always caused friction between the parties involved, and it affects the children. What else can we do so that stress does not overtake us? No matter who you talk to, no two divorces are the same. As I stated before, I had the opportunity to talk to several people about their experience with getting a divorce. It is good if you can depart and stay friends, but some divorces are devastating because they get the children involved, which isn't good at all. It brings hatred among the children and leaves them thinking it is their fault as they are pulled between both parents. There are things that are taught that could be true, but why mess with the children's minds. The children wind up having to get counseling because of the bad advice from the divorced parent. The children will learn on their own who the responsible party is, whether it is wrong or right. I know because I had to tell a woman that she shouldn't say anything negative about her husband as the children would learn on their own. Also, this way, the children do not have to go through unnecessary pain. Sometimes people will give unnecessary advice, but ensure you get the right advice. Friends mean well, but sometimes without knowing the truth, they can give the wrong advice. Seek a counselor. In the Bible, Job's friends had good intentions, but they did not know what Job was going through and why he was going through it. Job's friends heard of all the evil that came upon him, and they came to comfort him, but they didn't know what was wrong (Job 2:11). Job had friends who wanted to help and comfort him, which was good, but by not knowing the situation, they really didn't know how to help. That's how our friends are, we can appreciate it, but after their problem-solving, nothing helps. Now what? So how do we handle it? Come unto me, all who are ladened and a heavy laden, and I will give you rest. "Take my yoke upon you, and, and learn from me, but I am gentle and lowly in heart, and you will find ways for your soul, for my yoke is easy and my burden light." Matt. 11: 28-30

Remember that the sun will shine and there will be peace for you. God said in all things to give thanks; do this in bad times and good times. There is a reward for those that hold out until the end, it is a promise, and God cannot and will not lie (1 Thes 5:18 and Numbers 23:19). There can be concerns about remarrying. I was brought up in a church that taught that you don't divorce or remarry because the Bible stated that God hates divorce (Malachi 2:16).

But we have to study more into this scripture. It is set in the Old Testament, and God did give an order to protect the rights of divorcees (Deut 24:1-4) because of the hardness of people's hearts (Matt. 19: 8). Jesus came to save us from our sin, and God's grace and mercy help us today through Jesus Christ. Get wisdom and understanding through God and not man. I learned that man-made religion is legality much of the time because it is man-made. Now what? Let's get more into the word of God.

The truth about divorce is that it is never pretty even if both ends are agreeable; it is a nightmare. It has ended, and it feels like someone dies. Some people tried marriage counseling, but there is still no chance of salvaging the marriage as love is lost. Let me share my story so you can understand that it is not your fault. Stop it! Stop blaming yourself right now! I was married for thirty years, and I prayed and asked God, "why?" Sometimes it just happens; it didn't have to do with a man or woman. I think that we just grew apart. Our children were grown and had moved out except one. It didn't seem like there was anything else left. I do give him credit for taking care of his family, unlike some men. I felt like I was never appreciated. The "what now" I did was I went to hair school to get an education, hoping to find a job, which I did (I never had to work before. I was a stay home mom). After that, I finished college (Jackson State University) and got an associate degree. I didn't stop there; I went to a four-year college (Union university— Yeah to Union!) I got a degree in social work (a Bachelor's degree). I wasn't a young woman, so you see, you can do it too. I prayed on my bed after my divorce and cried, and it was like God said, "what are you crying for? Now get up and praise God for his goodness!" And that was what I did. I have been doing good ever since. I worked 13 years, and now, I am retired. I feel I had a productive life. I'm now a transitional coach; I teach a virtual class on whatever God leads me to teach. Now an author of two books and this one. God supplies my needs.

"You may ask anything in my name and I will do it" (John 14:14). Now, what is your "Now What"?

Have you ever faulted yourself about what caused your divorce? No, what are you doing about it?

_____

_____

_____

_____

_____

_____

_____

_____

Mary Thompson

Notes:

"Divorce is one of the most financially traumatic things you go through. Money spent on getting mad or getting even is money wasted."
- Richard Wagner

CHAPTER 4

STORMS OVERTURNING YOUR FINANCES

The phone rings, "Hello, is this Miss Livingston?" "Yes." "This is Check Into Cash. We have a deal today. Would you like to come in today? We have a deal that will last for only this weekend. You can get $200 today and skip one month's payment, but you would have to do it before the weekend." I want you to realize the play on the mind. You will find yourself robbing Peter to pay Paul, an old saying because it keeps you in debt. You keep telling yourself that you won't go back and that you are going to stop, but they use a good sales tactic that you can't resist. I've been there, done that. It's nothing that I am just saying. People lose their cars because they can't keep up with the payment. The Bible says, "owe no man anything" (Rom. 13:8). It is a form of slavery because we are always in debt to the person we owe (Prov 22:7 and (Deut 28:43-44). It is so easy to borrow money but hard to pay it back. Every time I borrowed money, it got harder and harder to get it paid back. In order to get out, I made a promise to a friend that I would never borrow money from Check into Cash again or any other similar service. I made that promise and was determined until I got out of debt. I also promised God if he would help me, I would never borrow money again from those cash advance places. I kept my promise. Yes, it was hard; I tell you no lie, but I was determined no matter what. I did not want to get a loan anymore of any kind because they know you will eventually get in trouble trying to pay them back, and then they will repossess your car. They don't care about how you get them paid; they just want to be paid. We need to remember that if we believe, God will meet our needs (Philippians 4:19). But God expects something from us too; we are expected to give also. God loves a cheerful giver, and when we give freely, it will come back to us. "Give, and it will be given to you. They will pour into your lap a good measure, pressed down, shaken together, and run over" (Luke 6:38). We must believe God's promise, and we must draw closer to him if we expected to see God work. I look back at my life, and I wonder how I made it over. God always provided. Even when I had to pay for things I wasn't expecting, I still had money that I didn't realize I had. It's like the scriptures say,

God will open the windows of heaven and pour out a blessing that you have no room to receive (Malachi 3:10). Because I pay my tithes, I don't worry about what people say; I do what I think will please God. People will try to stop you, but you can't listen to them. They only stop your blessing. Talk to God about your finances, and practice to be a good steward over your money. Get help from someone that you can trust to get your finances in control. Yes, it may cost you, but if you want to be financially able, it will help you to get your credit better and in control. Stop spending over your means; save your money until you can buy what you want and need. It hurts to be without, but you must train your children also to be patient with you until you can get them what they want. Help them to understand the situation you are in; they need to learn to appreciate what you are doing for them at this present time. Yes, it hurts when you can't get your children what they need, but they will understand if you teach them that it will come. I won't even go shopping because I feel like I will see something I want and can't buy it, and it makes me feel bad, so I stay away from those stores. The Bible says, "for which of you, intending to build a tower, sitteth not down first, and counteth the cost, whether he has sufficient to finish?" (Luke 14:28). We must learn to stay within our budget. You can't be like the Joneses; just be you and don't be ashamed. Again, teach your children to appreciate what they have so you won't feel hurt when you cannot get them what they want. Money can lead you the wrong way if you just want it and don't have it. For the love of money is the root of all kinds of evil. Some people, eager for money, have wandered from the faith and created for themselves many griefs (1 Tim 6:10). There are people in jail because they have gotten money in the wrong way, drugs, money laundering, theft, etc. Don't even let your mind wander. It is why there are a lot of divorces and separation. I go to the Bible when there is something that I need, to know that it will help me and keep my life from the love of money. It will help with being content with what you have, for he has said, "I will never leave you nor forsake you" (Hebrew 13:5). God will always be with us, he will send the help we need, but we must be faithful and stand on God's promises. God made promises for those that need him. Man has messed up what God has put together to benefit those that are in need. "Upon the first day of the week let every one of you lay by him in store, as God has prospered him, that there be no gathering when I come" (1 Corinthians 16:2). It was to be put aside to help those that are in need. You still see a little of this but not as much. You first need to do some research if you need help. It is out there for you. Did you lose your job? Don't think you can't bounce back; just don't give up.

I always say you wobble, but you get up. Just don't lay there. Don't be like the Ostriches and stick your head in the sand. A winner never quits, and quitters never win. Don't let your failures get you down. Though he may stumble, he will not fall, but the Lord upholds him with his hand (Psalm 37:29)

There are books and consultants that can help you get in touch with your financial life and credit. You have to have a mind to change. Be accountable for yourself. You can be debt-free and have financial freedom, but it takes time and motivation. Learn to invest and save your money. I watch my son learn all he could about investing in the stock market—something he was never taught at a younger age. So, there is no excuse for not trying. He now has his own business and a family of five. Don't fool yourself; you can't be lazy and expect to have true freedom. I had another son who stepped out on faith to build his business, working for others now working for himself. Both were told to give the 10% to God, and they have been teaching their children the same. It pays to be charitable (2 Cor 9:7) and to give God his 10 percent of tithes. "Will a man rob God? Yet ye have robbed me. But ye say, Wherein have we robbed thee? In tithes and offerings" (Malachi 3:8).

Did you take any fault for your dilemma? How have you corrected the situation?

Notes:

"Money never made a man happy yet, nor will it. The more a man has, the more he wants. Instead of filling a vacuum, it makes one."
- Benjamin Franklin

CHAPTER 5

QUIETNESS IN THE STORM OF LONELINESS

Have you ever sat in the night and it was so quiet that you couldn't hear anything but the wind blowing and the light rain on the rooftop? After being married for 30 years, then the divorce, with no children around, just me and the emptiness, wishing I had someone to cuddle up with. All I heard was someone telling me that it'll alright and that I'll meet someone else. Still, time goes on and on. Everyone got someone to go to. I will go to dinner and just stay at home and watch a movie. You even hear preachers saying you have sinned because of your thoughts of wanting someone as a companion. Come on now, what is the matter with them? They are married and have someone at home to share life with. Now don't get me wrong; the word I speak is not to give you an excuse to run out and commit fornication because that is a sin (1 Corinthians 6:18). We get lonely, and people say to wait on it. It seems hard to wait, but we must realize that we are the temple of God. We have to ask God to help when we are feeling lonely. He is the only one that can help us. I am not saying it is easy; it is not. Don't let anyone tell you it is. It's a matter of getting your focus on Jesus. I remember, at a young age, working in the church and being in prayer, there were a lot of sisters that wanted husbands. It was so bad that they testified that they set up a table for dinner for their husband to be there, trying to have faith that he would be there soon. Have you ever done that? Well, it kept them believing. I was told that you had to put yourself in a position to receive. Wow! Do you understand the Bible when it comes to believing in the word like we are supposed to? How do you take this scripture "who so findeth a wife findeth a good thing, and obtain a favor of the Lord" (Prov 18:22)? Does that mean you wait, or you make a way for him to find you? Have respect for yourself; don't jump for anything that looks like gold and has a good shine to it. The word does say he who finds a good wife finds a good thing and obtains favor of the Lord. You find favor of the Lord when you hear the word of the Lord; in all your ways, trust in the Lord, and he will supply you with a good wife or husband if that is His will. Sometimes, we want things that are not what God wants. Still, we keep asking, and God, knowing that it is not the best, lets you have it. Then He has to deliver us out of what we thought we wanted. Yes, it seems lonely being by yourself when everyone around you has someone to talk with. I get lonely; then I get lonely again and again. But God, full of grace, helps us when we call on him. If you are not careful, loneliness can have a stronghold (2 Cor10:4). Who out there, because you are lonely, started going on dating sites? Me. Yes, I did, but God revealed something to me that put me to shame. I am telling you that I spent money to find someone. That is not safe. Yes, there seem to be some success stories to be told, so I wouldn't say there are always bad stories to tell but let God direct you. It is said in his word that God will direct your path (Prov 3:6). The things I encountered were awful. I quickly knew this was not for me. I share this with you, so you don't be led the same way. It took me a while to get focused on God and his righteousness. It doesn't mean that you have sinned because God's grace is sufficient, and he is there to show us that he is the way. Seek you first the kingdom and his righteousness, and these things should be added to you (Matthew 6:33). You may wonder why Christians get lonely when we believe in God and have the hope that God is with us. Well, think about it. Some go to a non-caring church that does not see loneliness as a problem. Some do not want to share their feelings because they are afraid of how it will look like being a Christian, but Christians also suffer from loneliness. As long we live, we will have feelings of loneliness. You are not alone; get focused on God. I worked in mental health for 13 years and saw what loneliness can do to people—they shared the pain of being disconnected, overlooked, suicidal. God does not want you to think that way. God is still with you. Jesus even cries to the father, "my God, my God, why have you forsaken me? (Matt. 15:34). So, don't beat yourself up; being lonely is nothing to worry about. Loneliness is only bad when you don't know how to handle it.

Pray to God. "turn to me and be gracious to me, but I am lonely and afflicted, believe the trouble of my heart and free me from my anguish" (psalms 25:16, 17). You can be lonely for a wife, a husband, friendship, or family. Pray about it because if you are lonely, you should learn not only to survive but thrive. As Maya Angelou said, to do so with some patience, some compassion, some humor and some style. Here are some things that you can use when you are feeling lonely you can: (1) read a good book, (2) listen to some music, (3) volunteer to help someone else, (4) meditate on God's word, (5) get some counseling if it's extreme. Keep yourself busy as having a pity party will destroy you because Satan, the devil, would like to sift you as wheat and kill you (Luke 22:31-34). I want you to read this scripture and to know it is the truth. I want you to put your name in the blank, and after you read it, say, "not me, Satan, in Jesus' name." Here we go, say it with faith,

"But the Lord said_____,_____ behold, Satan hath desired to have _____,that he may sift _____as wheat.

"And my God shall supply all your need according to His riches in glory by Christ Jesus" (Phil 4:19)

Have you put your mind toward God when he said flee youthful lust? Yes? No? Not yet?

Notes:

We are all born alone and that alone. Loneliness is definitely part of the journal of life.
- Joni a Chen

CHAPTER 6

CLIMATE CHANGE IN THE STORM OF MENTAL HEALTH

The impact of climate change affects mental health. There is a lot to learn and understand about mental health. We must continue to study and research things about how to help. I have worked in the field for 13 years and have learned a lot. Hence, I understand the changes in a person's mind. My mother, bless her, was affected by mental illness. She was the sweetest person alive, and her respect for others was beyond and above beautiful. No one really knew about climate change and the impact on people. Now, slowly it is being studied and the effect it has on people. These studies show there is something going on with a person's health, more than asthma or allergies, but illness and injury related to storms. I am glad to see that psychologists are seeking out more information about climate change. It is said that climate change has effects on stress, depression, anxiety, and it is known to increase aggressiveness, violence, and crime. Climate change can threaten anyone, especially those dealing with a mental health condition. This is known by psychologists; it's a decision that has to be recognized by those that are doing the research now. Exposure to certain climate, weather, and natural disasters can result in mental illness, depression, or post-traumatic stress disorder, which can be led to chronic psychological issues, especially for high-risk people, children, women postpartum mothers, people who have a pre-existing mental illness, and people who are economically disadvantaged and homeless. Researchers are talking about climate change more due to the extreme heat effect on physical and mental health, raising disease and death rate because many psychotic medications impact the body's ability to regulate temperature. When my client comes into the office and we talk about stress and health, they say it bothers them when it is cloudy and dark out, and they feel more depressed. I would tell them to put on all the lights in the house because I recognize that being in the dark affects your mood. Even when I lived in Michigan, where it is cloudy all the time as there wasn't much sunlight, I always made a statement about this. I am so glad that people are looking into climate change. Mental illness is like standing in a snowstorm. It is like heavy snow that makes everything inconvenient, damages your relationships and families until everything seems to collapse. We need to get help and not be ashamed. Don't let people look down on you; hold your head high. I have a granddaughter that didn't let anything bother her. I admire her for not letting anyone get her down. She is a sweet and innocent teenager. When you try to bully her, she just looks at you with a look that says, "is that all you got?" (It's not funny, but she handles it). There are a lot of challenges you go through, but don't give up. God will fight your battle. My granddaughter was involved in a program that was called "Different and not Ashamed" this organization was very encouraging. They help many small children and adolescents become mentally intelligent. Look in your local paper or library for health providers or programs to give you resources for help. Mental illness is a disorder; it's not contagious. There is help, but we need to renew our minds (Roman 12:2). God gives us perfect peace when we keep our minds on Christ. It's nothing wrong with searching out professional help. We have been told so many negative things about mental illness that we are ashamed to let people know that we have issues in our lives that we are trying to handle alone. We don't need to handle this ourselves—not at all! You are not crazy; don't let no one tell you that either! This is the word that doesn't need to be stated. There are stories in the Bible that let you know that mental illness just didn't start; it has been here a long time. Matthew 17:5, "but God was there for him and his father because of his faith he was healed through faith." There are many ways of healing. There are doctors, therapies, and medicines, so believe in how God wants to heal you. Mental health is a disorder, and it is real. It can be treated. There are storms of health disorders in people's families, and when you don't know what to say or how to help someone, you should ask questions to help. They are having difficult times as well as you because their hands are tied. It feels like more than climate change. What can you do? Please don't self-diagnose anyone and give meds to them. Be supportive with children. Assist a person in seeing the physician. Remember, you are not a doctor. Just be there to support and help when they are in need.

"The real test is not whether you avoid this failure, because you won't. It's whether you let it harden or shame you into inaction, or whether you learn from it; whether you choose to persevere." —Barack Obama

Do you feel shame for someone close to you because of a mental disorder? And how can you correct it?

_____

_____

_____

_____

_____

_____

_____

_____

_____

_____

I have a number for you to call if you would like 1-800-662-Help (4357)

CHAPTER 7

THUNDERSTORMS IN LIFE/SUNSHINE IN DEATH

"And the Lord God formed man of the dust on the ground, and breathed into his nostrils the breath of life; and man became a living soul" (Gen 2:7). Sometimes, we look at life and wonder why we are here. We think of a lot of things as questions flow through our thoughts. Why? Because to some of us, we wonder, why do I have to be poor? Why can't I have a good job? Why do I have to work hard to get where I am going? Why can't I find true love? There are all these whys. Some of us go to church: some of us don't. Those that go to church learn to depend on God; those that don't do not know God because no one told them about God. So, some things are alright; at least they pretend it is. People think that life is having everything material here on earth. But that is not life; life is when you have sought God. "But seek you first the kingdom of God, and his righteousness; and all these things shall be added onto you" (Matthew 6:33). I had to learn that money isn't everything. My aunt always told me that if I have food on the table and clothes on my back, I should be satisfied. I had a friend growing up that would come to my house and be bragging all the time about what she had and what her father was buying her, whether it was a purse, shoes or TV. I got tired of her bragging. I grew up to learn that these things don't make you happy, but what makes a person happy is being committed to God, who breathes into us and gives us life. We live by the promises of God that will provide us everything we need. It may not seem to be what we want because the world makes things appear to be alright. We live because of God. "All the commandments which I command thee this day, shall ye observe and do; that he may live" (Deut 8:1). I want you to learn to live in Christ. When I was young, I just followed the format I was given about life and serving God. (1 Kings 19:4), "but he who himself went a day's journey into the wilderness and came and sat down under a Juniper tree: and he request for himself that he might die; and said, it is enough; now, o Lord, take away my life; for I am not better than my father." This is the story of Elijah. Let us know that things in life get hard; so hard that we want to die, and he was a prophet. Any of us can be that way; that's just you. See the big picture of life; there is hope at the end of the rainbow, so what will you do? Get up, my brother, my sister. Begin to live and consider your Juniper tree as a place you can go to refresh and think things out. Whether it be a friend or the closet or bathroom to pray, take to talking to God again. Hold on! Don't be like Peter when he walked on the way he was alright until he took his eyes off the Lord and began to sink (Matt 14:27-31). We cannot live life by ourselves; we need Jesus. Elijah realized he couldn't do anything on his own. When he was weak, God became his strength. He also can become our strength. God is the one that gives life, and he is the one that can take it away (Genesis 2:7). There are so many people who want to commit suicide; they don't realize Satan wishes to sift them as wheat. Luke 22:31, "Satan has desired to have you, that he may sift you as wheat." Satan just comes to rob, steal, and kill. (John 10:10), "The thief the (devil) comes to kill and destroy. Christ came to give us life." Although life is in God's hand, there is life after death. It is in God's hands that we live.

If we are in Christ, we shall live again. Death is something we never get used to. One day God will put death away; he has victory over death when he died on the cross and rose from the grave. There will be no more tears or sorry, crying or pain. They will be gone forever, and God will make everything new (Revelations 21:4). I cannot imagine a life without Christ! Who can say no to someone that has given their life for us, who prayed to his father that he did not lose any of us? This He did for us, that we will live right and live again! (John 17:1-26) I want you to understand that it is time to prepare yourself for the Lord to come. "We are confident, and willing whether to be absent from the body and to be with thee" (Phil 1:23).

Let's listen to this testimony. I am sure we have heard this saying that a parent should never have to bury a child. Well, I did. My oldest daughter passed away in 2009 from complications of kidney failure. I had so many emotions from sadness, denial, anger, and the "why" (my questioning God). How could God take this beautiful young lady from us, this young mother of four children? I began reading articles about mothers that have lost children, hoping that would help to ease my pain. In fact, I did read one where a mother explained how losing her daughter brought her closer to God. I began to realize that I should be praying for his guidance and strength rather than question God. I needed to be strong and be there for my grandkids. My prayers must have been answered because slowly, although the pain wasn't so heavy, I began to smile again. I learned a powerful lesson, to never doubt and always put God first. Gwendolyn Thompson, Memphis, Tennessee.

Seven years ago, I lost my baby. I had twins; the other twin was very sick and stayed in the hospital for six months. It was a very tough six months. Doctors stated that she would never walk, read, or do anything that normal children do. She was born 26 weeks early. It hurt so bad

(I even blamed myself). I grew up knowing God, and I had a praying mother and father. I was lost for a while, "But God." I thought about things, and of course, I did question God, but He was right there with me. I could have lost my mind, "But God." I held on to my faith in God. He brought me through. My baby is now 13 years old and doing great! Just like all the other kids. I know I will see my other baby again in heaven. To God be the glory. Charity Armstrong, Murfreesboro Tn.

Have you ever said these things to anyone that has lost someone, even when the Bible says you had to rejoice when someone dies and cry when a baby is born?

One. I know how you feel.

Two. You can always have other children.

Three. At least he is in a better place now.

Four. God never gives us more than we can handle.

Five. At least he or she lived a long life.

Six. Be strong; don't cry.

Seven. It was God's will; everything happens for a reason.

If you have gone through this, it has been said several times. People say things without thinking how it affects your feelings. Don't take it personally. Sometimes people don't really know what to say when something like this happens because death is devastating. So, let's learn from our mistakes.

Very truly, I tell you, whoever hears my word and believes him who sent me has eternal life and will not be judged but have crossed over from death to life. (John 5:24). I plead guilty of doing the same thing, but through life, I've learned (It is what we are taught). People have mentally lost it, so be careful what you say. Would you like to know how I know these things? Well, it's because I have gone through them. These words have been said to me, but I appreciate the concern that the people had for me. I lost a child in 1969 at age one year, a month and a day. You talk about a storm; oh my God, that was a storm for me. It was devastating, and I had no one to really talk to about my son's death. I was very young; I was 19. I couldn't talk to my mother; she was already hurting herself. She never knew that I blamed her. I really didn't want to talk to her. To tell the truth, I was angry with God also. But when I came to my senses, God was there with me in my hurt. God gave me enough time to realize that he was with me. After I thought about it, I realized my mother loved my baby as much as I did. I said to myself it was as much my fault as it was hers because I could have taken my son with me when I moved, but I was giving myself time to get settled in a new place. My mother hurt as much as I did. I then said to myself, it's no one's fault. It's just happened; we don't know when our time is up, but it truly is a right saying to know God is coming soon.

We have been saying this for a long time, but I thank God that he has given me an understanding of what he is talking about, that soon is when our time is up on this earth. So when is your soon? We just need to be ready. The word says we must rejoice when a person dies and cry when a baby is born. It took me years to really remember this and what it meant, but I did not cry for about two years after my son passed, but I thank God that I will see him again because I will live for Christ. I thank God I can share this testimony with my readers. God is with us, and he will keep us. He will return to this earth, and our spirit will return to God (Ecclesiastes 12:7). God will wipe all our tears away. We must get ourselves together and stop letting Satan think he has won by using our story of death to take our minds. We have to hold on and never give up fighting it with the help of God's strength.

I even watched my granddaughter pass away. She was only one pound and four ounces. I watched her as she passed away, so I know what death is about. I know what a person goes through; I know what people say when they try to comfort you. My words are true, and I want to give you hope to live for Christ today. Be strong and of good courage for your God love you. I want to leave this thought with you. In Psalms, David said:

"The Lord is my shepherd; I shall not want, He makes me lie down in green pasture, He leads me beside the still waters. He restores my soul. He leads me in the paths of righteousness for his name's sake. Even though I walk through the valley of the shadow of death, I will fear no evil for you are with me; your rod and your staff, they comfort me, You prepare a table before me in the presence of my enemies, you anoint my head with oil; my cup runneth over. Surely goodness and mercy shall follow me all the days of my life, and I shall dwell in the house of the Lord forever" (Psalms 23). And this is my now what! I plan to serve God until I die, and I know I will be with him, and I will see all my loved ones that have gone on again. Life is what you make it. We have it so hard because we look at the "Joneses," and our minds wander off until it gets us in trouble. Let's stop. Look in the mirror and say to yourself, "I can, and I will."

Whomsoever hears my word and believe him who sent me has eternal life and will not be judged but have crossed over from death to life (John 5:24)

Death and life are in the power of the tongue (Prov 18:21)

Have you ever said these statements yourself?

_____

_____

_____

_____

After The Storm, Now What?

How will you correct them?

Notes:

"Death is nothing else but going home to God, the bond of love will be unbroken for all eternity."
-Mother Theresa

CHAPTER 8

AFTER THE STORM, NOW WHAT?

We have lived. We have gotten up. We have had faith, and now for those lacking faith, ask God for help and wait on him. I finally understood now. The old testament is the type in the shadow of things to come. As I study God's word, it shows clearly that the end time is approaching. God's judgment is coming; will you be ready? Revelation shows it all. God has a plan and a purpose for your life, "for I know the thoughts that I think toward you, says the Lord, thoughts of peace and not of evil, to give you a future and a hope" (Jer at 29:11). In your darkest hour, remember that God was and is with you. In time there will be more than just peace here on earth but always in heaven. Let's learn to pray. During this pandemic, I have learned a lot; God has opened things that we should see and know that he is a true and living God. Let God take control; he has got it all in his hands. We are more than conquerors through Christ Jesus (Rom 8:37), and there is treasure at the end of the rainbow. We see that if we only let God take control of our life, He will hide us in His loving arms, and we will be OK. Remember that this God is glorified in everything that we do righteously by him. Now what? Now is to believe God for everything; everything is pointing to the end. There will be a new heaven and earth. If our name is written above in the Lamb's book of life, we will be with Jesus in the kingdom of God. Now, what happens to the people that testified about their storm? Now what? Julia Gauthia is still doing good, and when things flare up, she doesn't give up. She lives by faith in God. She has a positive attitude. She said a good attitude and a man that did not give up helped her through the day. Now she and her husband have a productive life. She has great-grandchildren that she loves and takes care of and she just thank God for all that He has been to her. Her favorite scripture to use is "nay, in all things we are more than conquerors through him that loves us" (Roman 8:37).

Charity Thompson is raising her two girls and expecting a new baby boy in 2021. She is happy, and now her daughter that wasn't expected to live, is 13. Charity is so grateful to the Lord. Her preteen is doing good in school and other activities, running, walking, and playing on her tablet. Teachers say that she is an adorable child. Her mother gets a kick out of all those things she sees her daughter doing that they say that she will never do. Charity said, "it's amazing all my daughter can do."

Charity thanks God. She said that she walks by faith and sight—"but we walk by faith and not by sight" (ll Cor 5:7).

Gwen Thompson stated that she put her trust in God. She is so thankful that she learned to trust God and understands that God has a plan for her. Gwen says that she is watching her grandchildren grow up, which gives her joy. They are doing good, and by grace, she says, "I can do all things through Christ who strengthens me" (Philippians 4:13).

Tammy Thompson is now enjoying family and about to move into a two-bedroom house. From being homeless and having to live with a family member to now having her housewarming party with family and friends. Thanking God for everything, she sends her love to everyone that stood by her and showed her love. Married to her husband for 18 years, she thanks her husband for all his support. Tammy thanks you all and stated that "y'all Rock!" "Thank God for everything because it was through him that I live, and I am enjoying life. To this day. I shall not die but live and declare the works of the Lord." (Ps118:17)

Now you can see that all these people who have given you a testimony now live a productive life, living for Christ. All is well, thanks to Jesus Christ, who has helped them see everything through. And the same thinking can happen to you if you only believe and trust in God; he is with you all the time. You can be more than a conqueror, and you can do all things through Christ Jesus, who gives you the strength. What he has done for one, he can do for the other. But Christ never changes; he is the same yesterday, today and forever. But God knows that the plans you have for us that we will prosper and be in good health, so why not just try God today and put him through the test, and he will show us what he can do. Whatever you have chosen to do within your life, now that you have gone through all the trouble you have, you can choose what you will and do it, believing in God. After my storms, I have had praise in my heart, and you can also have praise in your heart and magnify God for his glory. But we have always been put here to praise God and to glorify him. Think about your life, now what?

God gives us peace. He is the same yesterday, today, and forever. You can and will have a beautiful life. This is YOUR NOW WHAT! "But I know the plans I have for you, declares the Lord, plans to prosper you and not to harm you, plans to give you a hope and a future" Jeremiah 29:11.

Now, what will you do after the Storm?

Notes:

"When you are in the middle of a storm cloud, it's hard to think outside of it. But the only way out of the storm is to read through it and things will be a lot clearer on the other side."

-Jodi Ann Bickley

CHAPTER 9

NOW WHAT? CONTINUE...

The reflection of our past is looking in the mirror, seeing ourselves and wanting a better life. A refraction of change of direction that you are going through just like the rainbow. (We are living in type and shadows of things to come) I think about the old patriots in the old and New Testament and about what they did when they had hard storms of life that came against them. For instance,

Daniel in the lion's den, Joseph sold into slavery, how Job suffered, the three Hebrew boys, and Saul. Although we go through a lot and wonder whether God is still there with us through the storm, he just wants us to hold on. I had to learn on my own, but hopefully, this book as you read will help you. I believe what I write because I have been there. We are more than conquerors through Christ Jesus (Rom 8:37). If we hold on, God will keep his promise, don't let anyone discourage you (Is. 40:31). There's a crown for us all, and if we trust God and live for him, we can receive his number in our hand and head as Relation states (Rev7:3) that shows that we belong to him. Never give up and continue to hold on. After you have suffered, then comes the end, and now what? There is eternal life that awaits us. Let's look at the patriots of old and see what a blessing they received after they waited on Jesus after that they had suffered and went through. Daniel was a faithful servant; even when he was thrown in the lion's den, he believed in God. That's what we need—more faith to trust God. God sent an angel to protect him. So, you see, God will do the same for us (Heb 13:8). Take Joseph, for example; he was sold into slavery by his brother because of their jealousy because of the vision God had given him. His brother did not like what Joseph told them about the beautiful colorful coat God was going to give him and about God making him a ruler. Look what happened to him; he had to depend on God and remained steadfast. God's grace will help us in our time of need. Joseph suffered a loss from his father, believing he was dead and his brothers' plot. God has a plan for your life. Just remain strong and steadfast. God sees and knows everything. He is there to bring us out. In Gen 37, after what Joseph went through, he was made the second most powerful man in Egypt next to the pharaoh. There's a plan for us after we have suffered a while, and if we hold out, God has a plan for me and you. I am fulfilling His purpose for you by writing to you so that you can hold on. Think about Job, Job was a wealthy man, and he was everything, so to speak. Wealth does not make you happy; after the wealth is gone, now what? Who do you have to depend on? Job did not think about God being there with him because of all that he was going through. Job was blameless and upright; what could he have done to bring such sickness on himself? And as it is, there is Satan who comes to try him. Satan just comes to steal and kill and take your life; everything was taken from Job. Job even wanted to die. His friend even talked about him. God already told Satan he could not have his soul. After holding on, Job was blessed to get everything he had back. Job's wife even told him to curse God, but after he suffered for a while, God was there. You might wonder to yourself, why did all this happen to Job? God just asks you to believe. There is a reward for us; just hold on. We do not understand everything that comes upon us; that is why it is important to hold on. I cannot say it enough because so many people are suffering through the storms of life and getting weary. The Bible said that you did run well and what did hinder you (Gal 5:7). Now let's look as we reflect, looking at the Hebrew boys. These boys refused to bow down before the king and worship his god. The king gave an order that if they did not bow down their heads when they heard the music, they would be punished. The same is today; we want everything but God. Whatever you encounter today, God is able to get you out of it. The trouble you may have seems hard, and you can't do anything about it. Yet, let it go and let God help you. He said to be patient and wait on Him to get you out of your financial troubles, divorce, life and death, loneliness, anything that has you bound. Don't be tempted by others that make you feel bad about things that you have no control of. The Hebrew boys believed that whatever the king do to them, their God would get them out. I love it when the king looked into the furnace and saw not only three in the furnace but four (Dan 3:24-25)—it was the son of God. Hallelujah! Believe me, God is with you wherever you are in life. Stand still and see the salvation of God. Exodus 14:3-15 is just a few verses in the Bible that talk about tribulation, which is storms in life that come without warning. I am trying to encourage you to read God's word and get some deliverance for your soul. Receive God before it is too late, and you are destroyed in your storms. God is giving all of us a chance. Revelation states that "there were two men will be in the field, one will be taken and the one will be left. Two women will be grinding in at the well, one will be taken and the one will be left (Matt 24:40). This is just to let you know after everything you have gone through and what will happen next, now what? Think of these things as your pot of gold at the end of the rainbow, waiting to be received.

Where there is no vision, the people perish (Prov 29:18)

What is your vision for life?

Three things you expect from God.

Notes:

> "Many of life's failures are people who do not realize how close they were to success when they gave up."
> - Thomas A. Edison

CHAPTER 10

AFTER THE STORM, THERE IS A POT OF GOLD AT THE END OF THE RAINBOW

There is a saying that there is a pot of gold at the end of the rainbow. People understand that no one had ever gotten to the end of the rainbow, so they never reached the end (this is an idiom, a group of words established by usage as having a meaning not deducible from those of the individual words, a google search). But in Christ, we always look for hope and happiness. Rainbows are motivation for us to continue to believe in these times. The fact about the rainbow is that it is thought of as good fortune. We know God will bring us hope for God's promises. Even though rainbows are myths, God's word is true. The rainbow is God's promises, and His word is like gold, so we look for his promises, and in reference to the gold, we are looking for His promises. We have sunshine and rain to make a rainbow. Let me explain to you what a rainbow is. It's a phenomenon caused by reflection, refraction and dispersion of light in water droplets resulting in a spectrum of light appearing in the sky (Basic Wikipedia Dictionary). He will never leave us. But there is sunshine after the rain. We face our challenges, and we are more than conquerors if we believe and hold on to our faith. We search for the word of God that gives us that hope (our pot of gold). There is a story in the Bible that God told Noah and his son that he would establish a covenant with him and with the seed after him that he wouldn't use water to destroy the earth, but he would set his bow in the clouds, which shows a promise kept because the Rainbow is still there today to show God's promises and they are true (Gen 6:13), (Num 23:19), (l Samuel 15:29), (Heb 6:18). We have God's word, which is our pot of gold that we can hold on to in the time of the storms. God is Real, and we must believe that when the storms hit so hard, he is there amid it. Remember the three Hebrew boys put in the furnace that wouldn't bow and worship another god, and the king looked in and saw four instead of three? So, you see, God is there with us, and he is with us even when we do not see him (Daniel 3). We search for many things, but do we search for the word of God (our goal) in the Bible? As humans, we have to believe in something. Without a vision, a man perishes. Even the rainbow gives us hope because it is the promise of God. Have you ever seen people's reactions when they see a rainbow in the sky? They say, "Oh, God, there is a rainbow!" They get excited because of God's promise. When I was a child, I visualized going to the end of the rainbow to get my pot of gold. I had no idea where to start because I didn't know where to go, when I finally thought I was there, it was gone. I feel like if I had the pot of gold, it would have taken care of a lot of problems, especially financially. I kept my hope as I grew up. Then I found out the real story of the rainbow, as I had stated above (they are God's covenants to man because of the flood). There is still hope at the end of the rainbow. We know that we cannot reach it because the rainbow is never-ending. It's like it goes through the earth and connects as a whole. This just lets you know there is a God that keeps his promise. Let's look at the colors of the rainbow and see what it says. Green is a sign of life and hope. Blue is water which is for life drawn up by the clouds from the sea. Yellow brings laughter and gaiety into the world. Orange is the color of health and strength; although it may be scarce; it serves the inner need of human life. Red is like blood—the color of passion and love. Purple is royalty and power. Our treasure wrapped up in Jesus, our goal, all put together. 1 John I:7, "but if we walk in the light, as he is in the light, we have fellowship one with another, and the blood of Jesus Christ, his son, cleanses us from all sin." A promise to his people that he is with us. A son of hope for today, tomorrow and forever. (Have you ever thought about how colors matter?)

"I am continuously inspired by nature, and the rainbow is one of nature's greatest optical phenomena. The sighting of a rainbow never fails to bring a smile to people's faces. They signify optimism and positivity; with them comes the sunshine after the rain." Matthew Williamson

Questions about your storm

How do you see your storms now?

What and how can you help yourself to get through your storms?

How can Jesus help you in your storms?

Say it;

Believe it;

Receive it;

Watch for Jesus blessings

If you don't know Jesus for the remission of your sins, do this and be born again that if thou shalt confess with your mouth the Lord Jesus, and shalt believe in thine heart that God has raised Him from the dead, thou shall be saved.

Romans 10:9

Notes:

References from King James Version

Storm	Divorce	Finance	Life/death
Matt 8:24	Deut 22:19	Eccl 5:10	GN 2:7
Mk 4:37	1 pt 3:1	Deut 8:18	GN 50:1-11
Jn 6:18	Gn2;24	Matt 6:24	Jn 20;22
Lk 7:46-49	Matt 5:32-3	Prov 13:11	Ps 23:4
Ps 107:28-31	Jer 3:1	Prov21;5	GN 4:8-10
Ps 55:16-8	Rom 7:2-3	Lk 14:28	1 Cor 3:22
Nahum 1:7	Ex 14:14	Prov 30:24	Jn 1:12-13
Job 38:1-6	Deut 22:19	Cor 9;6-8	Phil 1:20
Deut 31:8	Heb 13:4	Deut 15:7	Rev 21:4
Is 28:12	1 Pt 3:1	Act 20:25	1 Cor 15:16
Ps 91:1-5	Is 1:17	James 5:4	1 Tim 6:12
2 Cor 4:8-10	Eph 5:33	Prov 14:23	Rom 5:11

Other References on God's promises

Gen 9:13-16	Rev1:1	Ezekiel 1;29	Rom 8:18
Rev 4:3	Rev 4:1-11	Isa 58;8-10	Debut 7;9
Ps 23:1-6	Gen 9:9-14	Gen 9:15-17	Rev4:1-4
Ez 1:26-28	Rev 10: 1-2	2 Thess 3:3-4	Isa 6:3
1 Cor 1:8-9	1 Thes 5:24	Prov 3:5-6	Rom 8:28
Josh 1:9	Rom 8:18	Is 6:3	Lament 3:21-26

CHAPTER 11

FINALLY, THE END OF THE STORMS

In reality, our storms would be over mentally and spiritually. As we say, we all get caught up in life, but as I write, I could not end this book without letting you know that after the storm, now what? Without letting you know that regardless of all you face (your own storms), there will be peace, love, and humility, no more crying, weeping, miseries, any such thing. We will be able to celebrate a new life with God for eternity. There will be light in your darkest hour here and now and afterward. If you just keep the faith and HOLD on again and again. It is better than waiting on $1 million. This is the end of your storm spiritually. Jesus is coming soon. When I was young, I kept hearing people say God is coming soon. They would pack up their stuff and give it to the pastor (now what sense does that make). I am sure you have heard that saying before. If you are older, you would know; if you are younger, ask someone older. This went on for a long time, and people are still saying, "well, I've been around for a long time, and I haven't seen him yet."

They mock the Scriptures because they are ignorant (meaning they just don't know). Well, I will tell you now what God gave in Revelations 22:7 BEHOLD, I COME QUICKLY: blessed is he that keeps the sayings of the prophecy of this book (mean in the Bible)". "Soon" does not mean right now. We should live each day learning about Jesus and his return any day. God showed me that soon can be at the time he calls you home, like right now your time is up. He wants us to be ready because right then is your soon. Have you given God your life?

Have you given God your life by repenting and being ready? We don't know how much longer our life will be. Waiting for Jesus to take on a sense of urgency—"soon." Whether or not

"soon" means today; let's be faithful today to remember these words and learn from God's word what it means. God is real and true about what He says, we only know in parts. 1 Corinthians 13:12 says, then I shall know fully, even as I have fully known. We shall see it clearly. Just be ready when he comes, both physically and spiritually. He said he was coming soon; as it is said, get your house in order.

Act 3: 19 says, repent ye therefore and be converted that your sins may be blotted out.

Act 2:38, Peter said unto them, Repent, and be baptized every one of you in the name of Jesus Christ for the remission of your sins.

Matt 4:17, Jesus began to preach, and say, Repent for the kingdom of heaven is at hand.

I do not claim to know everything, but I do know what God is saying. Be strong, hold on, and he is coming soon.

Study God's word to find out the ending and beginning of life. Jesus is coming. He is the Alpha and Omega, the first and the last, the beginning and the end. Do not add or take away God's words (Revelation 22:18). Surely, I will come quickly. Amen. Even so, come, Lord Jesus. The grace of the Lord Jesus be with you all.

Let Pray:

Our Heavenly Father, thank you for life and more abundance of our faith in your word. Let us keep it close to our heart as we see the ending of all our storms, looking for a fresh beginning and saving according to your word. I repent of all my sins and believe that Jesus Christ died for my sin by shedding his blood. I confess to you now. I thank you right now in the name of Jesus. Amen. Amen. Amen.

If you know Jesus was coming soon how would this change your life?

_____

_____

_____

_____

_____

_____

How would you be living if Jesus knocked on your door right now?

Now what would you do to better your life to be ready if the "soon" was now?

www.ingramcontent.com/pod-product-compliance
Lightning Source LLC
LaVergne TN
LVHW051841080426
835512LV00018B/3003